The Power of Art and Symbols
For Activism in Kenya

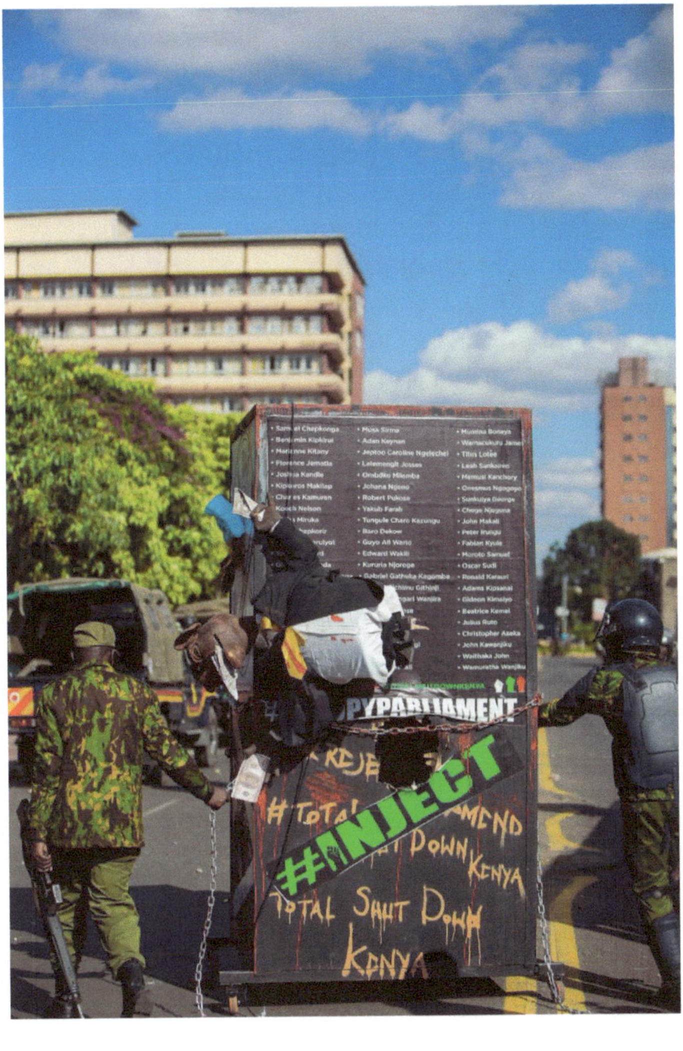

Written by Fedelis Kyalo

Preface

"The Power of Art and Symbols for Activism in Kenya" examines the significant role of art and symbols in driving social and political movements, especially considering corruption and public dissatisfaction with governance. It reveals how diverse groups, including doctors, lecturers, university students, and Gen Z activists, have come together via protests demanding accountability.

In Kenya, puppetry has become an innovative method for promoting education and social change, notably through the influential television satire "The XYZ Show."

This book discusses the use of creative symbols in demonstrations, such as oversized pigs and postal boxes, which illustrate public dissent against corrupt practices and specific legislation.

Ultimately, this book asserts that art remains a powerful vehicle for advocating good governance and highlights the relentless efforts of citizens striving for accountability and transparency in Kenya, framing this movement as crucial for the nation's future.

Historically, art has served as a powerful instrument in protests worldwide. Movements like Occupy Wall Street, which began in the U.S. in 2011, showed how large symbolic images can effectively communicate messages to both the government and the public.

Inspired by Spain's 15-M movement, these protests used striking visuals to create memorable and resonant statements, proving that art can amplify voices and shape narratives. In Kenya, puppeteers have harnessed the power of puppetry as a tool for education and social change.

For over 30 years, talented puppeteers have engaged communities through entertaining and informative shows that address important issues such as good governance, health concerns, and environmental conservation.

The use of puppets in education has proven to be an effective way to communicate complex messages in a relatable and accessible manner.

The impact of puppetry in Kenya grew even more significant when it transitioned to television. The introduction of the popular political satire "The XYZ Show" marked a turning point. This show cleverly targeted the political class, using humor and satire to hold politicians accountable and keep them in check.

With its engaging content, "The XYZ Show" quickly gained a massive following, and puppetry began to be appreciated in a new light.

Politicians themselves became fans of the show, with some even requesting their characters to be introduced, while others sought to have their portrayals removed, fearing damage to their reputations.

President Ruto was among the notable characters featured, illustrating the show's influence in political discourse.

As the tradition of using puppets in governance evolved, it subsequently found its way into protests. From the original "Occupy Parliament" protest in 2019 to the more recent demonstrations in June of 2024, the role of puppetry has become increasingly prominent in activism.

This year, Gen Z and activists made a historic move by storming the Parliament building, marking a significant shift in the landscape of activism in Kenya.

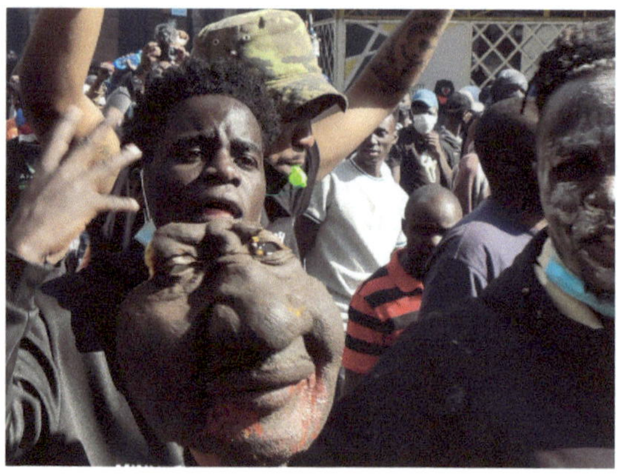

This bold action signified a turning point, especially since previous attempts to reach Parliament had been met with resistance. The integration of puppetry into protests has allowed activists to convey their messages in creative and impactful ways.

Puppets have become symbols of dissent, engaging audiences and drawing attention to pressing issues. As the movement continues to expand, puppeteers play a vital role in shaping the narrative around governance and societal change in Kenya.

A key aspect of these protests has been the creative symbols that emerged. Protesters have employed oversized pigs to symbolize corrupt members of Parliament, giant boxing gloves to represent the fight against corruption, and large babies in diapers to illustrate the immaturity of some politicians.

They have also used massive bullets to highlight police violence and coffins to mourn victims of abductions.

One of three predominant symbols that emerged during the protests was a giant suitcase measuring 4ft by 2ft. The suitcase, created during the first week of June, represented the rejection of a controversial finance bill that many criticized for potentially raising taxes and burdening ordinary Kenyans.

Generation Z and other bold activists mounted the suitcase on a cart and rolled it through the streets on the day MPs voted on the bill. Police quickly confiscated it.

In mid-June, a second compelling symbol emerged during the protests: a large postal box, measuring 4ft by 4ft, encircled with chains and boldly labeled "Return to Sender." Signs attached to the box proclaimed, "We reject the bill." This box was more than just an object; it represented the collective voice of the protesters who wanted to send a clear message to the government about their discontent with the controversial finance bill.

Activists chained themselves to the box, demonstrating their commitment to the cause and their determination to stand firm against the bill. However, as the protests escalated and chaos erupted, the situation quickly became dangerous. The air filled with tear gas, making it difficult to breathe. Realizing the intensity of the situation, the activists had no choice but to unchain themselves and flee for their safety.

The protests during this time were marked by intense confrontations. The atmosphere was charged with frustration and urgency as citizens sought to make their voices heard. Running battles broke out across the Central Business District (CBD), with police attempting to control the crowds and block access to Parliament. Thousands of people had turned out to voice their concerns, but despite their numbers, they were never allowed to reach the Parliament building. The postal box served as a poignant symbol of the protesters' desire to send the finance bill back to Parliament and urge President Ruto to not sign it.

After the activists abandoned the postal box amidst the chaos, police quickly confiscated it and towed it away, leaving many feeling disheartened. The loss of this symbol was a blow to the protesters who had poured their energy and creativity into the demonstration. However, the activists' efforts were not in vain.

The widespread protests and the strong message conveyed by the postal box captured public attention and put pressure on the government. Ultimately, the president responded to the outcry and returned the bill for further review, signaling that the voices of the people were being acknowledged.

This development highlighted the power of collective action and the importance of symbols in advocating for change, reminding everyone that even in the face of adversity, their voices can make a difference.

The third symbol, created on June 25, 2024, was a large 8ft by 4ft replica of the parliament building. Sitting atop the replica was a pig puppet holding a stack of money, showing the greed of the MPs who supported the finance bill. Below the pig was a puppet of President Ruto's face, which people could easily slap.

The puppets looked like those from the popular TV show, The XYZ Show, which many Kenyans loved. Though the show was off the air due to the struggling economy, its impact on the lives of Kenyans was unmistakable. The replica was designed to be big and easy to move, with wheels that could easily roll through the streets.

It quickly became the main attraction, visible from afar. Merely constructed in two days by puppet makers and graffiti artists, the replica incorporated messages and names of 195 lawmakers who supported the finance bill. As protesters marched, many took turns slapping the president's puppet while calling him "Mwizi" (thief), creatively demonstrating their anger.

Protesters took control of the city's central business district causing many businesses to close. Police responded by shooting at the crowd with tear gas and water cannons. During the course of the day-long demonstration, many young protesters were killed by police. Some of them suffered serious injuries, including head wounds. The majority of casualties occurred outside of the parliament building when protesters overpowered the police and rushed inside. MPs were quickly taken through a secret tunnel to the basement of their new building, where they stayed until police regained control. Many MPs were injured in the chaos, and the mace (a symbol of authority for Kenya's parliament) was stolen and broken in two.

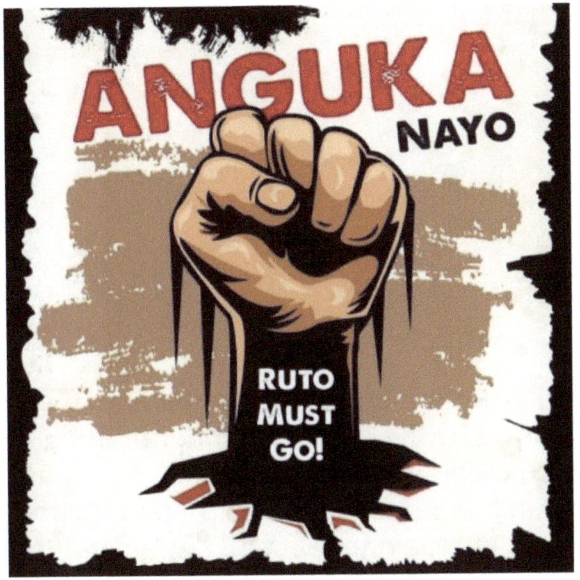

By the time police restored order in Parliament, everything was in shambles—windows were broken, flags were stolen, chairs were scattered, and fires were ignited. Thick clouds of tear gas filled the agitated air, disguising the parliament replica. As bodies piled up on the ground, only a few determined people continued protesting. From a distance, the pig puppet could still be seen on top of the replica, serving as a haunting reminder of the protests' original purpose. The once busy streets were now almost empty, a sharp contrast to the lively energy that had filled them just moments before.

Many observers believed that the fires were not started by the protesters but rather by hired goons looking to incite further mayhem and discredit the movement. The protesters had aimed to maintain a peaceful demonstration, highlighting the stark divide between their intentions and the violent reality that unfolded.

Sadly, the final images of the puppet replica were disheartening. When the police seized it, the pig puppet was tilted awkwardly to the side and the puppet of the president's head had been ripped apart. This was symbolic of the deep frustration of Gen Z and the intense anger and disillusionment of the people, who had grown tired of the president's leadership only two years after the elections.

What started as a creative and hopeful protest turned into a tragic situation filled with violence and loss. Despite the tragic deaths that day, Gen Z played a vital role in rallying support for the protests. They skillfully used social media to spread the 'Occupy Parliament' message by sharing posters and making videos on TikTok and Facebook. This drew global attention to the situation in Kenya, with celebrities worldwide joining in and dancing to the protest song "Anguka Nayo", which means "going down with the protest," along with the rallying slogan "Ruto Must Go".

Gen Z infused the movement with new energy. They sported coordinating outfits while sharing important information online leading up to the event. Their efforts resulted in a vibrant display of unity and determination as they took to the streets, demanding the removal of the finance bill, the resignation of all cabinet secretaries, and the ousting of President Ruto for failing to fulfill his development promises. In response, Ruto initially removed all cabinet secretaries and rejected the finance bill. However, just two weeks later, he reinstated most of them and formed a coalition with the opposition to undermine the Gen Z movement.

Despite the creativity and profound impact of these protests, they continue to face significant challenges.

Police crackdowns have become increasingly common, as authorities work to suppress dissent by confiscating artistic symbols and disrupting gatherings. Many forms of artistic expression have been destroyed or seized, and there have been reports of abductions, with artists and activists being taken by masked security personnel from the streets and their homes. Surveillance tactics, including the tracking and bugging of mobile phones, create an atmosphere of fear. In response to this oppressive environment, many are turning to social media platforms like X (formerly Twitter), TikTok, and Facebook, transforming them into virtual spaces for civic education. These platforms are enlightening the public about stalled government projects, exposing corruption, and sharing contact information for corrupt politicians, encouraging people to "Salimia yeye" (greet him/her).

Art has proven to be an effective medium for advocating good governance in Kenya, turning protests into unforgettable and impactful events. As citizens continue to take to the streets, employing innovative symbols and creative expressions, the hope for a more accountable and transparent government remains vibrant. The struggle for justice through art is not merely a fleeting moment; it is a powerful movement aimed at reshaping the future of governance in Kenya. Through their unwavering resilience and ingenuity, the people of Kenya are making it clear that they will not be silenced. Unwaveringly, they assert that their demands for change will continue to echo throughout the streets.

~ ~ ~

<u>**Notes & Ideas**</u>

<u>Notes & Ideas</u>

Notes & Ideas

<u>Notes & Ideas</u>

<u>**Notes & Ideas**</u>

Notes & Ideas

Notes & Ideas